See the bright blue sky?
What else is blue?

Hear the red birds sing?
What else is red?

Feel the cool green grass?
What else is green?

Smell the sweet yellow flowers?

What else is yellow?

What a colorful world!

The Best Book of
Volcanoes

Simon Adams

KINGFISHER

BOSTON

Contents

Created for Kingfisher Publications Plc
by Picthall & Gunzi Limited

Author: Simon Adams
Consultant: Dr. Jon French,
University College, London
Editor: Karen Dolan
Designer: Dominic Zwemmer
Editorial assistance: Barnaby
 Harward
Illustrators: Rob Jakeway,
 Bill Donohoe

KINGFISHER
a Houghton Mifflin Company imprint
222 Berkeley Street
Boston, Massachusetts 02116
www.houghtonmifflinbooks.com

First published in 2001
First published in this format in 2007
10 9 8 7 6 5 4 3 2 1

1TR/0906/SHENS/PICA(PICA)/126.6MA/F

LIBRARY OF CONGRESS CATALOGING-IN-PUBLICATION DATA
has been applied for.

ISBN 978-0-7534-6092-4

Printed in Taiwan